9/16

Little Pebble™

Construction Vehicles at Work

BULLDOZERS

by Kathryn Clay

raintree

a Capstone company — publishers for children

Raintree is an imprint of Capstone Global Library Limited, a company incorporated in England and Wales having its registered office at 264 Banbury Road, Oxford, OX2 7DY – Registered company number: 6695582

www.raintree.co.uk
myorders@raintree.co.uk

ISBN 978 1 4747 2719 8
20 19 18 17 16
10 9 8 7 6 5 4 3 2 1

British Library Cataloguing in Publication Data
A full catalogue record for this book is available from the British Library.

Editorial credits
Erika L. Shores, editor; Juliette Peters and Kayla Rossow, designers;
Eric Gohl, media researcher; Tori Abraham, production specialist

Photo credits
Alamy: ZUMA Press Inc, 7; iStockphoto: kozmoat98, 9; Shutterstock: artiomp, cover, bogdanhoda, 11, f9photos, 5, TFoxFoto, 1, 13, 15, 17, 19, Vadim Ratnikov, 21

Design elements: Shutterstock

Printed in China.

Contents

About bulldozers

Look!

Here comes a bulldozer.

Lee is the driver.

He sits in the cab.

cab

CAT

D5G LGP

CAT

Here is the blade.

It pushes soil.

blade

The blade is strong.

It is steel.

Here are the tracks.

There are two.

track

track

13

Tracks go over hills.

Tracks go through mud.

At work

Thud!

Clear a path.

Push down trees.

Rocks and sand get
pushed away.
Now the land is flat.

Here is the new road.

Well done, bulldozer!

Glossary

blade   wide, curved piece of metal; the blade pushes or scrapes rocks and soil

cab   place where the driver sits

track   metal belt that runs around wheels

Find out more

B is for Bulldozer, June Sobel (Houghton Mifflin Harcourt, 2013)

Bulldozers (Mighty Machines), Amanda Askew (QED Publishing, 2011)

Machines on a Construction Site (Machines at Work), Sian Smith (Raintree, 2014)

Websites

www.ivorgoodsite.org.uk/
Meet Ivor Goodsite, and learn all about safe construction sites.

www.toddlertube.co.uk/things-that-go/things-that-go-movies.html
The Things That Go! website has all kinds of videos about construction vehicles, including a video showing how roads are made.

Index